Our Daily B

2019 Planner

PERSONAL INFORMATION

Name:

Address:

City: State: Zip:

Home Phone: Cell Phone:

Work Phone:

Discovery House
from Our Daily Bread Ministries

Scriptures taken from the Holy Bible, New International Version®, NIV®. Copyright © 1973, 1978, 1984, 2011 by Biblica, Inc.™ Used by permission of Zondervan. All rights reserved worldwide. www.zondervan.com. The "NIV" and "New International Version" are trademarks registered in the United States Patent and Trademark Office by Biblica, Inc.™

Design by Sherri Hoffman

Cover photo: Darrell Gulin

Printed in the United States of America

2019

January 2019
S	M	T	W	TH	F	S
		1	2	3	4	5
6	7	8	9	10	11	12
13	14	15	16	17	18	19
20	21	22	23	24	25	26
27	28	29	30	31		

February 2019
S	M	T	W	TH	F	S
					1	2
3	4	5	6	7	8	9
10	11	12	13	14	15	16
17	18	19	20	21	22	23
24	25	26	27	28		

March 2019
S	M	T	W	TH	F	S
					1	2
3	4	5	6	7	8	9
10	11	12	13	14	15	16
17	18	19	20	21	22	23
24	25	26	27	28	29	30
31						

April 2019
S	M	T	W	TH	F	S
	1	2	3	4	5	6
7	8	9	10	11	12	13
14	15	16	17	18	19	20
21	22	23	24	25	26	27
28	29	30				

May 2019
S	M	T	W	TH	F	S
			1	2	3	4
5	6	7	8	9	10	11
12	13	14	15	16	17	18
19	20	21	22	23	24	25
26	27	28	29	30	31	

June 2019
S	M	T	W	TH	F	S
						1
2	3	4	5	6	7	8
9	10	11	12	13	14	15
16	17	18	19	20	21	22
23	24	25	26	27	28	29
30						

July 2019
S	M	T	W	TH	F	S
	1	2	3	4	5	6
7	8	9	10	11	12	13
14	15	16	17	18	19	20
21	22	23	24	25	26	27
28	29	30	31			

August 2019
S	M	T	W	TH	F	S
				1	2	3
4	5	6	7	8	9	10
11	12	13	14	15	16	17
18	19	20	21	22	23	24
25	26	27	28	29	30	31

September 2019
S	M	T	W	TH	F	S
1	2	3	4	5	6	7
8	9	10	11	12	13	14
15	16	17	18	19	20	21
22	23	24	25	26	27	28
29	30					

October 2019
S	M	T	W	TH	F	S
		1	2	3	4	5
6	7	8	9	10	11	12
13	14	15	16	17	18	19
20	21	22	23	24	25	26
27	28	29	30	31		

November 2019
S	M	T	W	TH	F	S
					1	2
3	4	5	6	7	8	9
10	11	12	13	14	15	16
17	18	19	20	21	22	23
24	25	26	27	28	29	30

December 2019
S	M	T	W	TH	F	S
1	2	3	4	5	6	7
8	9	10	11	12	13	14
15	16	17	18	19	20	21
22	23	24	25	26	27	28
29	30	31				

2020

January 2020
S	M	T	W	TH	F	S
			1	2	3	4
5	6	7	8	9	10	11
12	13	14	15	16	17	18
19	20	21	22	23	24	25
26	27	28	29	30	31	

February 2020
S	M	T	W	TH	F	S
						1
2	3	4	5	6	7	8
9	10	11	12	13	14	15
16	17	18	19	20	21	22
23	24	25	26	27	28	29

March 2020
S	M	T	W	TH	F	S
1	2	3	4	5	6	7
8	9	10	11	12	13	14
15	16	17	18	19	20	21
22	23	24	25	26	27	28
29	30	31				

Contributors' Bios

Terry Bidgood has served as graphics manager for more than twenty years at Our Daily Bread Ministries. Terry's photographs have appeared on the covers of *Our Daily Bread*, the Discovery Series booklets, and on Discovery House music and book products. He has traveled extensively, taking photographs in locations as diverse as South America, New Zealand, the Grand Canyon, and the Holy Land.

A committed *Our Daily Bread* reader, world-class photographer **Darrell Gulin** has seen his photos featured on many of the devotional's covers. Gulin's photos—captured in widespread places around the globe—are distributed by top agencies that sell them for use in magazines, catalogs, and other publications. For Darrell, "It's an extra blessing to capture nature and wildlife on film and show others just how wonderful God's creation is."

Chek Phang (C. P.) Hia brings a distinctive flavor to *Our Daily Bread*. He and his wife, Lin Choo, reside in the island nation of Singapore. C. P. came to faith in Jesus Christ at the age of 13. During his early years as a believer, he was privileged to learn from excellent Bible teachers who instilled in him a love for God's Word. He currently serves in the Singapore office as special assistant to the Our Daily Bread Ministries president. He and his wife enjoy traveling and going for walks. They have a son, daughter-in-law, grandson, and granddaughter who also live in Singapore.

Amy Peterson teaches at Taylor University. She has a B.A. in English Literature from Texas A&M and an M.A. in Intercultural Studies from Wheaton College, and is completing an M.F.A. through Seattle Pacific University. Amy taught ESL for two years in Southeast Asia before returning stateside to teach in California, Arkansas, Washington, and Indiana. She is the author of *Dangerous Territory: My Misguided Quest to Save the World*. Amy enjoys reading, quilting, hiking, and experimenting in sustainable practices of living.

Amy Boucher Pye is a writer and speaker who lives in North London. She's the author of the book *The Living Cross: Exploring God's Gift of Forgiveness and New Life* and the award-winning book *Finding Myself in Britain: Our Search for Faith, Home, and True Identity*. She runs the Woman Alive book club in the UK and enjoys life with her family in their English vicarage. Find her at amyboucherpye.com or on Facebook or Twitter (@amyboucherpye).

David Roper was a pastor for more than thirty years and now directs Idaho Mountain Ministries, a retreat dedicated to the encouragement of pastoral couples. He enjoys fishing, hiking, and being streamside with his wife, Carolyn. His favorite fictional character is Reepicheep, the tough little mouse that is the soul of courage in C. S. Lewis's Chronicles of Narnia series. His favorite biblical character is Caleb—that rugged old saint who never retired, but who "died climbing."

Alex Soh is a firm believer in the power of photography to communicate ideas and emotions. He desires to capture the wonders of nature that will compel people to worship its wonderful Creator. As art director for Our Daily Bread Ministries' international operations, he has been building the organization's stock image library since 1997. His photographs have won numerous international awards and accolades. You can find more of his work at alexsohphotography.com.

Breath of Life

Then the LORD *God . . . breathed into his nostrils the breath of life.*
GENESIS 2:7

O n a cold and frosty morning, as my daughter and I walked to school, we enjoyed seeing our breath turn to vapor. We giggled at the various steamy clouds we could each produce. I received the moment as a gift, reveling in being with her and being alive.

Our breath, which is usually invisible, was seen in the cold air, and it made me think about the Source of our breath and life—the Lord our Creator. For He who formed Adam out of the dust of the ground, giving him the breath of life, also gives life to us and to every living creature (Genesis 2:7). All things come from Him—even our very breath, which we inhale without even thinking about.

We may be tempted, living with today's conveniences and technology, to forget our beginnings and that God is the one who gives us life. But when we pause to remember that God is our Creator, we can build an attitude of thankfulness into our daily routines. We can ask Him for help and acknowledge the gift of life with humble, thankful hearts. May our gratitude spill out and touch others, so that they also may give thanks to the Lord for His goodness and faithfulness.

—AMY BOUCHER PYE

Dear heavenly Father, what an awesome and powerful God you are! You created life by your very breath. We praise you and stand in awe of you. Thank you for your creation.

2019

JANUARY

Sunday	Monday	Tuesday	Wednesday
		1 New Year's Day	2
6 Epiphany	7	8	9
13	14	15	16
20	21 Martin Luther King Jr. Day	22	23
27	28	29	30

Neither height nor depth, nor anything else . . .
will be able to separate us from the love of God
that is in Christ Jesus.   —ROMANS 8:39

Thursday	Friday	Saturday	Notes
3	4	5	
10	11	12	
17	18	19	
24	25	26	
31			

Shopping List

January 2019

S	M	T	W	TH	F	S
	1	2	3	4	5	
6	7	8	9	10	11	12
13	14	15	16	17	18	19
20	21	22	23	24	25	26
27	28	29	30	31		

February 2019

S	M	T	W	TH	F	S
					1	2
3	4	5	6	7	8	9
10	11	12	13	14	15	16
17	18	19	20	21	22	23
24	25	26	27	28		

2018–2019

DEC–JAN

Sunday 30

Monday 31 New Year's Eve

Tuesday 1 New Year's Day

Wednesday 2

Thursday 3

Friday 4

Saturday 5

To-Do List

✓

Shopping List

January 2019						
S	M	T	W	TH	F	S
		1	2	3	4	5
6	7	8	9	10	11	12
13	14	15	16	17	18	19
20	21	22	23	24	25	26
27	28	29	30	31		

February 2019						
S	M	T	W	TH	F	S
					1	2
3	4	5	6	7	8	9
10	11	12	13	14	15	16
17	18	19	20	21	22	23
24	25	26	27	28		

2019

JANUARY

Sunday 6 Epiphany

Monday 7

Tuesday 8

Wednesday 9

Thursday 10

Friday 11

Saturday 12

To-Do List

Shopping List

January 2019

S	M	T	W	TH	F	S
		1	2	3	4	5
6	7	8	9	10	11	12
13	14	15	16	17	18	19
20	21	22	23	24	25	26
27	28	29	30	31		

February 2019

S	M	T	W	TH	F	S
					1	2
3	4	5	6	7	8	9
10	11	12	13	14	15	16
17	18	19	20	21	22	23
24	25	26	27	28		

2019

JANUARY

Sunday 13

Monday 14

Tuesday 15

Wednesday 16

Thursday 17

Friday 18

Saturday 19

To-Do List

Shopping List

January 2019
S	M	T	W	TH	F	S
		1	2	3	4	5
6	7	8	9	10	11	12
13	14	15	16	17	18	19
20	21	22	23	24	25	26
27	28	29	30	31		

February 2019
S	M	T	W	TH	F	S
					1	2
3	4	5	6	7	8	9
10	11	12	13	14	15	16
17	18	19	20	21	22	23
24	25	26	27	28		

2019
JANUARY

Sunday 20

Monday 21   Martin Luther King Jr. Day

Tuesday 22

Wednesday 23

Thursday 24

Friday 25

Saturday 26

To-Do List

✓

Shopping List

2019

JAN-FEB

Sunday 27

Monday 28

Tuesday 29

Wednesday 30

Thursday 31

Friday 1

Saturday 2 Groundhog Day

To-Do List

✓

2019

FEBRUARY

Sunday	Monday	Tuesday	Wednesday
3	4	5	6
10	11	12	13
17	18 Presidents' Day	19	20
24	25	26	27

Let the peace of Christ rule in your hearts.
—COLOSSIANS 3:15

Thursday	Friday	Saturday	Notes
	1	2 Groundhog Day	
7	8	9	
14 Valentine's Day	15 Flag Day (Canada)	16	
21	22	23	
28			

Shopping List

February 2019						
S	M	T	W	TH	F	S
					1	2
3	4	5	6	7	8	9
10	11	12	13	14	15	16
17	18	19	20	21	22	23
24	25	26	27	28		

March 2019						
S	M	T	W	TH	F	S
					1	2
3	4	5	6	7	8	9
10	11	12	13	14	15	16
17	18	19	20	21	22	23
24	25	26	27	28	29	30
31						

2019
FEBRUARY

Sunday 3

Monday 4

Tuesday 5

Wednesday 6

Thursday 7

Friday 8

Saturday 9

To-Do List

✓

Shopping List

February 2019

S	M	T	W	TH	F	S
					1	2
3	4	5	6	7	8	9
10	11	12	13	14	15	16
17	18	19	20	21	22	23
24	25	26	27	28		

March 2019

S	M	T	W	TH	F	S
					1	2
3	4	5	6	7	8	9
10	11	12	13	14	15	16
17	18	19	20	21	22	23
24	25	26	27	28	29	30
31						

2019

FEBRUARY

Sunday 10

Monday 11

Tuesday 12

Wednesday 13

Thursday 14 Valentine's Day

Friday 15 Flag Day (Canada)

Saturday 16

To-Do List

Shopping List

February 2019

S	M	T	W	TH	F	S
					1	2
3	4	5	6	7	8	9
10	11	12	13	14	15	16
17	18	19	20	21	22	23
24	25	26	27	28		

March 2019

S	M	T	W	TH	F	S
					1	2
3	4	5	6	7	8	9
10	11	12	13	14	15	16
17	18	19	20	21	22	23
24	25	26	27	28	29	30
31						

2019
FEBRUARY

Sunday 17

Monday 18 Presidents' Day

Tuesday 19

Wednesday 20

Thursday 21

Friday 22

Saturday 23

To-Do List

✓

Shopping List

February 2019

S	M	T	W	TH	F	S
					1	2
3	4	5	6	7	8	9
10	11	12	13	14	15	16
17	18	19	20	21	22	23
24	25	26	27	28		

March 2019

S	M	T	W	TH	F	S
					1	2
3	4	5	6	7	8	9
10	11	12	13	14	15	16
17	18	19	20	21	22	23
24	25	26	27	28	29	30
31						

2019
FEB-MARCH

Sunday 24

Monday 25

Tuesday 26

Wednesday 27

Thursday 28

Friday 1

Saturday 2

To-Do List

✓

MARCH

Sunday	Monday	Tuesday	Wednesday
3	4	5	6 Ash Wednesday
10 Daylight Saving Time Begins	11 Commonwealth Day (Canada)	12	13
17 St. Patrick's Day	18	19	20 First Day of Spring
24 31	25	26	27

The grace of God has appeared that offers
salvation to all people. —TITUS 2:11

Thursday	Friday	Saturday	Notes
	1	2	
7	8	9	
14	15	16	
21	22	23	
Purim			
28	29	30	

Shopping List

March 2019

S	M	T	W	TH	F	S
					1	2
3	4	5	6	7	8	9
10	11	12	13	14	15	16
17	18	19	20	21	22	23
24	25	26	27	28	29	30
31						

April 2019

S	M	T	W	TH	F	S
	1	2	3	4	5	6
7	8	9	10	11	12	13
14	15	16	17	18	19	20
21	22	23	24	25	26	27
28	29	30				

2019

MARCH

Sunday 3

Monday 4

Tuesday 5

Wednesday 6 Ash Wednesday

Thursday 7

Friday 8

Saturday 9

To-Do List

✓	

Shopping List

March 2019

S	M	T	W	TH	F	S
					1	2
3	4	5	6	7	8	9
10	11	12	13	14	15	16
17	18	19	20	21	22	23
24	25	26	27	28	29	30
31						

April 2019

S	M	T	W	TH	F	S
	1	2	3	4	5	6
7	8	9	10	11	12	13
14	15	16	17	18	19	20
21	22	23	24	25	26	27
28	29	30				

2019

MARCH

Sunday 10 Daylight Saving Time Begins

Monday 11 Commonwealth Day (Canada)

Tuesday 12

Wednesday 13

Thursday 14

Friday 15

Saturday 16

To-Do List

✓

Shopping List

March 2019

S	M	T	W	TH	F	S
					1	2
3	4	5	6	7	8	9
10	11	12	13	14	15	16
17	18	19	20	21	22	23
24	25	26	27	28	29	30
31						

April 2019

S	M	T	W	TH	F	S
	1	2	3	4	5	6
7	8	9	10	11	12	13
14	15	16	17	18	19	20
21	22	23	24	25	26	27
28	29	30				

2019

MARCH

Sunday 17 St. Patrick's Day

Monday 18

Tuesday 19

Wednesday 20   First Day of Spring

Thursday 21   Purim

Friday 22

Saturday 23

To-Do List

✓

Shopping List

March 2019

S	M	T	W	TH	F	S
					1	2
3	4	5	6	7	8	9
10	11	12	13	14	15	16
17	18	19	20	21	22	23
24	25	26	27	28	29	30
31						

April 2019

S	M	T	W	TH	F	S
	1	2	3	4	5	6
7	8	9	10	11	12	13
14	15	16	17	18	19	20
21	22	23	24	25	26	27
28	29	30				

2019

MARCH

Sunday 24

Monday 25

Tuesday 26

Wednesday 27

Thursday 28

Friday 29

Saturday 30

To-Do List

✓

Begin Where You Are

The heavens declare the glory of God;
the skies proclaim the work of his hands.

PSALM 19:1

I came across a solitary flower growing in a meadow today—a tiny purple blossom "wasting its sweetness in the desert air," to borrow from the poet Thomas Gray's wonderful line. I'm sure no one had seen this particular flower before, and perhaps no one will see it again. *Why this beauty in this place?* I thought.

Nature is never wasted. It daily displays the truth, goodness, and beauty of the One who brought it into being. Every day nature offers a new and fresh declaration of God's glory. Do I see Him through that beauty, or do I merely glance at it and shrug it off in indifference?

All nature declares the beauty of the One who made it. Our response can be worship, adoration, and thanksgiving—for the radiance of a cornflower, the splendor of a morning sunrise, the symmetry of one particular tree.

Author C. S. Lewis describes a walk in the forest on a hot summer day. He had just asked his friend how best to cultivate a heart thankful toward God. His hiking companion turned to a nearby brook, splashed his face and hands in a little waterfall, and asked, "Why not begin with this?" Lewis said he learned a great principle in that moment: "Begin where you are."

A trickling waterfall, the wind in the willows, a baby robin, the blue sky, a tiny flower. Why not begin your thankfulness with this?

DAVID ROPER

Father, may we always be reminded that you have placed beauty here because it reflects your character. We praise you!

Photo: Almond flower; Alex Soh
© Our Daily Bread Ministries

APRIL

Sunday	Monday	Tuesday	Wednesday
	1	2	3
7	8	9	10
14	15	16	17
Palm Sunday			
21	22	23	24
Easter Sunday	Easter Monday (Canada) Earth Day		
28	29	30	

Thursday	Friday	Saturday	Notes
4	5	6	
11	12	13	
18	19	20	
Maundy Thursday	Good Friday	Passover Begins	
25	26	27	
		Passover Ends	

Shopping List

April 2019

S	M	T	W	TH	F	S
	1	2	3	4	5	6
7	8	9	10	11	12	13
14	15	16	17	18	19	20
21	22	23	24	25	26	27
28	29	30				

May 2019

S	M	T	W	TH	F	S
			1	2	3	4
5	6	7	8	9	10	11
12	13	14	15	16	17	18
19	20	21	22	23	24	25
26	27	28	29	30	31	

2019

MARCH–APRIL

Sunday 31

Monday 1

Tuesday 2

Wednesday 3

Thursday 4

Friday 5

Saturday 6

To-Do List

✓

Shopping List

April 2019

S	M	T	W	TH	F	S
	1	2	3	4	5	6
7	8	9	10	11	12	13
14	15	16	17	18	19	20
21	22	23	24	25	26	27
28	29	30				

May 2019

S	M	T	W	TH	F	S
			1	2	3	4
5	6	7	8	9	10	11
12	13	14	15	16	17	18
19	20	21	22	23	24	25
26	27	28	29	30	31	

2019

APRIL

Sunday 7

Monday 8

Tuesday 9

Wednesday 10

Thursday 11

Friday 12

Saturday 13

To-Do List

✓

Shopping List

April 2019

S	M	T	W	TH	F	S
	1	2	3	4	5	6
7	8	9	10	11	12	13
14	15	16	17	18	19	20
21	22	23	24	25	26	27
28	29	30				

May 2019

S	M	T	W	TH	F	S
			1	2	3	4
5	6	7	8	9	10	11
12	13	14	15	16	17	18
19	20	21	22	23	24	25
26	27	28	29	30	31	

2019

APRIL

Sunday 14 — Palm Sunday

Monday 15

Tuesday 16

Wednesday 17

Thursday 18 Maundy Thursday

Friday 19 Good Friday

Saturday 20 Passover Begins

To-Do List

✓

Shopping List

April 2019						
S	M	T	W	TH	F	S
	1	2	3	4	5	6
7	8	9	10	11	12	13
14	15	16	17	18	19	20
21	22	23	24	25	26	27
28	29	30				

May 2019						
S	M	T	W	TH	F	S
			1	2	3	4
5	6	7	8	9	10	11
12	13	14	15	16	17	18
19	20	21	22	23	24	25
26	27	28	29	30	31	

2019

APRIL

Sunday 21 Easter Sunday

Monday 22 Earth Day
Easter Monday (Canada)

Tuesday 23

Wednesday 24

Thursday 25

Friday 26

Saturday 27 Passover Ends

To-Do List

☑

Shopping List

April 2019

S	M	T	W	TH	F	S
	1	2	3	4	5	6
7	8	9	10	11	12	13
14	15	16	17	18	19	20
21	22	23	24	25	26	27
28	29	30				

May 2019

S	M	T	W	TH	F	S
			1	2	3	4
5	6	7	8	9	10	11
12	13	14	15	16	17	18
19	20	21	22	23	24	25
26	27	28	29	30	31	

✓

2019
APRIL-MAY

Sunday 28

Monday 29

Tuesday 30

Wednesday 1

Thursday 2 National Day of Prayer

Friday 3

Saturday 4

To-Do List

✓

MAY

Sunday	Monday	Tuesday	Wednesday
			1
5	6	7	8
12	13	14	15
Mother's Day			
19	20	21	22
	Victoria Day (Canada)		
26	27	28	29
	Memorial Day		

[The Lord] does great things beyond
our understanding. —JOB 37:5

Thursday	Friday	Saturday	Notes
2 National Day of Prayer	3	4	
9	10	11	
16	17	18	
23	24	25	
30	31		

Shopping List

May 2019

S	M	T	W	TH	F	S
			1	2	3	4
5	6	7	8	9	10	11
12	13	14	15	16	17	18
19	20	21	22	23	24	25
26	27	28	29	30	31	

June 2019

S	M	T	W	TH	F	S
						1
2	3	4	5	6	7	8
9	10	11	12	13	14	15
16	17	18	19	20	21	22
23	24	25	26	27	28	29
30						

2019

MAY

Sunday 5

Monday 6

Tuesday 7

Wednesday 8

Thursday 9

Friday 10

Saturday 11

To-Do List

✓

Shopping List

S	M	T	W	TH	F	S
			1	2	3	4
5	6	7	8	9	10	11
12	13	14	15	16	17	18
19	20	21	22	23	24	25
26	27	28	29	30	31	

May 2019

S	M	T	W	TH	F	S
						1
2	3	4	5	6	7	8
9	10	11	12	13	14	15
16	17	18	19	20	21	22
23	24	25	26	27	28	29
30						

June 2019

2019

MAY

Sunday 12 Mother's Day

Monday 13

Tuesday 14

Wednesday 15

Thursday 16

Friday 17

Saturday 18

To-Do List

✓

Shopping List

May 2019						
S	M	T	W	TH	F	S
			1	2	3	4
5	6	7	8	9	10	11
12	13	14	15	16	17	18
19	20	21	22	23	24	25
26	27	28	29	30	31	

June 2019						
S	M	T	W	TH	F	S
						1
2	3	4	5	6	7	8
9	10	11	12	13	14	15
16	17	18	19	20	21	22
23	24	25	26	27	28	29
30						

2019

MAY

Sunday 19

Monday 20 Victoria Day (Canada)

Tuesday 21

Wednesday 22

Thursday 23

Friday 24

Saturday 25

To-Do List

Shopping List

May 2019

S	M	T	W	TH	F	S
			1	2	3	4
5	6	7	8	9	10	11
12	13	14	15	16	17	18
19	20	21	22	23	24	25
26	27	28	29	30	31	

June 2019

S	M	T	W	TH	F	S
						1
2	3	4	5	6	7	8
9	10	11	12	13	14	15
16	17	18	19	20	21	22
23	24	25	26	27	28	29
30						

2019

MAY–JUNE

Sunday 26

Monday 27   Memorial Day

Tuesday 28

Wednesday 29

Thursday 30

Friday 31

Saturday 1

To-Do List

2019

JUNE

Sunday	Monday	Tuesday	Wednesday
2	3	4	5
9 Shavuot Pentecost	10	11	12
16 Father's Day	17	18	19
23 30	24	25	26

*Sing to the L*ORD *a new song, his praise from*
the ends of the earth. —ISAIAH 42:10

Thursday	Friday	Saturday	Notes
		1	
6	7	8	
13	14	15	
	Flag Day		
20	21	22	
	First Day of Summer		
27	28	29	

Shopping List

June 2019

S	M	T	W	TH	F	S
						1
2	3	4	5	6	7	8
9	10	11	12	13	14	15
16	17	18	19	20	21	22
23	24	25	26	27	28	29
30						

July 2019

S	M	T	W	TH	F	S
	1	2	3	4	5	6
7	8	9	10	11	12	13
14	15	16	17	18	19	20
21	22	23	24	25	26	27
28	29	30	31			

2019

JUNE

Sunday 2

Monday 3

Tuesday 4

Wednesday 5

Thursday 6

Friday 7

Saturday 8

To-Do List

✓

Shopping List

June 2019						
S	M	T	W	TH	F	S
						1
2	3	4	5	6	7	8
9	10	11	12	13	14	15
16	17	18	19	20	21	22
23	24	25	26	27	28	29
30						

July 2019						
S	M	T	W	TH	F	S
	1	2	3	4	5	6
7	8	9	10	11	12	13
14	15	16	17	18	19	20
21	22	23	24	25	26	27
28	29	30	31			

2019

JUNE

Sunday 9   Shavuot
Pentecost

Monday 10

Tuesday 11

Wednesday 12

Thursday 13

Friday 14 Flag Day

Saturday 15

✓

Shopping List

June 2019

S	M	T	W	TH	F	S
						1
2	3	4	5	6	7	8
9	10	11	12	13	14	15
16	17	18	19	20	21	22
23	24	25	26	27	28	29
30						

July 2019

S	M	T	W	TH	F	S
	1	2	3	4	5	6
7	8	9	10	11	12	13
14	15	16	17	18	19	20
21	22	23	24	25	26	27
28	29	30	31			

2019

JUNE

Sunday 16   Father's Day

Monday 17

Tuesday 18

Wednesday 19

Thursday 20

Friday 21 First Day of Summer

Saturday 22

To-Do List

✓	

Shopping List

✓	

June 2019

S	M	T	W	TH	F	S
						1
2	3	4	5	6	7	8
9	10	11	12	13	14	15
16	17	18	19	20	21	22
23	24	25	26	27	28	29
30						

July 2019

S	M	T	W	TH	F	S
	1	2	3	4	5	6
7	8	9	10	11	12	13
14	15	16	17	18	19	20
21	22	23	24	25	26	27
28	29	30	31			

2019
JUNE

Sunday 23

Monday 24

Tuesday 25

Wednesday 26

Thursday 27

Friday 28

Saturday 29

To-Do List

✓

Mightier than All

The LORD reigns, he is robed in majesty;
the LORD is robed in majesty and armed
with strength.

PSALM 93:1

Iguazu Falls, on the border of Brazil and Argentina, is a spectacular waterfall system of 275 falls along 2.7 km (1.67 miles) of the Iguazu River. Etched on a wall on the Brazilian side of the Falls are the words of Psalm 93:4, "Mightier than the thunders of many waters, mightier than the waves of the sea, the LORD on high is mighty!" (RSV). Below it are these words: "God is always greater than all of our troubles."

The writer of Psalm 93, who penned its words during the time that kings reigned, knew that God is the ultimate King over all. "The LORD reigns," he wrote. "Your throne was established long ago; you are from all eternity" (vv. 1–2). No matter how high the floods or waves, the Lord remains greater than them all.

The roar of a waterfall is truly majestic, but it is quite a different matter to be in the water hurtling toward the falls. That may be the situation you are in today. Physical, financial, or relational problems loom ever larger and you feel like you are about to go over the falls. In such situations, the Christian has Someone to turn to. He is the Lord, "who is able to do immeasurably more than all we ask or imagine" (Ephesians 3:20), for He is greater than all our troubles.

C. P. HIA

Lord, I know that you are powerful and greater than any trouble that might come my way. I trust you to carry me through.

Photo: Havasu Falls, Arizona, US © Terry Bidgood

2019

JULY

Sunday	Monday	Tuesday	Wednesday
	1 Canada Day	2	3
7	8	9	10
14	15	16	17
21	22	23	24
28	29	30	31

Yes, my soul, find rest in God;
my hope comes from him.
—PSALM 62:5

Thursday	Friday	Saturday	Notes
4	5	6	
Independence Day			
11	12	13	
18	19	20	
25	26	27	

Shopping List

July 2019

S	M	T	W	TH	F	S
	1	2	3	4	5	6
7	8	9	10	11	12	13
14	15	16	17	18	19	20
21	22	23	24	25	26	27
28	29	30	31			

August 2019

S	M	T	W	TH	F	S
				1	2	3
4	5	6	7	8	9	10
11	12	13	14	15	16	17
18	19	20	21	22	23	24
25	26	27	28	29	30	31

2019

JUNE–JULY

Sunday 30

Monday 1 Canada Day

Tuesday 2

Wednesday 3

Thursday 4   Independence Day

Friday 5

Saturday 6

To-Do List

Shopping List

July 2019

S	M	T	W	TH	F	S
	1	2	3	4	5	6
7	8	9	10	11	12	13
14	15	16	17	18	19	20
21	22	23	24	25	26	27
28	29	30	31			

August 2019

S	M	T	W	TH	F	S
				1	2	3
4	5	6	7	8	9	10
11	12	13	14	15	16	17
18	19	20	21	22	23	24
25	26	27	28	29	30	31

2019

JULY

Sunday 7

Monday 8

Tuesday 9

Wednesday 10

Thursday 11

Friday 12

Saturday 13

To-Do List

✓

Shopping List

July 2019

S	M	T	W	TH	F	S
	1	2	3	4	5	6
7	8	9	10	11	12	13
14	15	16	17	18	19	20
21	22	23	24	25	26	27
28	29	30	31			

August 2019

S	M	T	W	TH	F	S
				1	2	3
4	5	6	7	8	9	10
11	12	13	14	15	16	17
18	19	20	21	22	23	24
25	26	27	28	29	30	31

2019

JULY

Sunday 14

Monday 15

Tuesday 16

Wednesday 17

Thursday 18

Friday 19

Saturday 20

To-Do List

✓

Shopping List

July 2019						
S	M	T	W	TH	F	S
	1	2	3	4	5	6
7	8	9	10	11	12	13
14	15	16	17	18	19	20
21	22	23	24	25	26	27
28	29	30	31			

August 2019						
S	M	T	W	TH	F	S
				1	2	3
4	5	6	7	8	9	10
11	12	13	14	15	16	17
18	19	20	21	22	23	24
25	26	27	28	29	30	31

2019

JULY

Sunday 21

Monday 22

Tuesday 23

Wednesday 24

Thursday 25

Friday 26

Saturday 27

To-Do List

✓

Shopping List

July 2019

S	M	T	W	TH	F	S
	1	2	3	4	5	6
7	8	9	10	11	12	13
14	15	16	17	18	19	20
21	22	23	24	25	26	27
28	29	30	31			

August 2019

S	M	T	W	TH	F	S
				1	2	3
4	5	6	7	8	9	10
11	12	13	14	15	16	17
18	19	20	21	22	23	24
25	26	27	28	29	30	31

2019

JULY–AUGUST

Sunday 28

Monday 29

Tuesday 30

Wednesday 31

Thursday 1

Friday 2

Saturday 3

To-Do List

✓

2019

AUGUST

Sunday	Monday	Tuesday	Wednesday
4	5	6	7
11	12	13	14
18	19	20	21
25	26	27	28

Lord my God, I take refuge in you.
—PSALM 7:1

Thursday	Friday	Saturday	Notes
1	2	3	
8	9	10	
15	16	17	
22	23	24	
29	30	31	

Shopping List

August 2019

S	M	T	W	TH	F	S
				1	2	3
4	5	6	7	8	9	10
11	12	13	14	15	16	17
18	19	20	21	22	23	24
25	26	27	28	29	30	31

September 2019

S	M	T	W	TH	F	S
1	2	3	4	5	6	7
8	9	10	11	12	13	14
15	16	17	18	19	20	21
22	23	24	25	26	27	28
29	30					

2019

AUGUST

Sunday 4

Monday 5

Tuesday 6

Wednesday 7

Thursday 8

Friday 9

Saturday 10

To-Do List

✓

August 2019						
S	M	T	W	TH	F	S
				1	2	3
4	5	6	7	8	9	10
11	12	13	14	15	16	17
18	19	20	21	22	23	24
25	26	27	28	29	30	31

September 2019						
S	M	T	W	TH	F	S
1	2	3	4	5	6	7
8	9	10	11	12	13	14
15	16	17	18	19	20	21
22	23	24	25	26	27	28
29	30					

2019
AUGUST

Sunday 11

Monday 12

Tuesday 13

Wednesday 14

Thursday 15

Friday 16

Saturday 17

To-Do List

Shopping List

2019

AUGUST

Sunday 18

Monday 19

Tuesday 20

Wednesday 21

Thursday 22

Friday 23

Saturday 24

To-Do List

✓

August 2019						
S	M	T	W	TH	F	S
				1	2	3
4	5	6	7	8	9	10
11	12	13	14	15	16	17
18	19	20	21	22	23	24
25	26	27	28	29	30	31

September 2019						
S	M	T	W	TH	F	S
1	2	3	4	5	6	7
8	9	10	11	12	13	14
15	16	17	18	19	20	21
22	23	24	25	26	27	28
29	30					

2019

AUGUST

Sunday 25

Monday 26

Tuesday 27

Wednesday 28

Thursday 29

Friday 30

Saturday 31

To-Do List

✓

2019

SEPTEMBER

Sunday	Monday	Tuesday	Wednesday
1	2 Labor Day Labour Day (Canada)	3	4
8	9	10	11
15	16	17	18
22	23 First Day of Autumn	24	25
29	30 Rosh Hashana		

Many, LORD my God, are the wonders you have done. —PSALM 40:5

Thursday	Friday	Saturday	Notes
5	6	7	
12	13	14	
19	20	21	
26	27	28	

Shopping List

September 2019

S	M	T	W	TH	F	S
1	2	3	4	5	6	7
8	9	10	11	12	13	14
15	16	17	18	19	20	21
22	23	24	25	26	27	28
29	30					

October 2019

S	M	T	W	TH	F	S
		1	2	3	4	5
6	7	8	9	10	11	12
13	14	15	16	17	18	19
20	21	22	23	24	25	26
27	28	29	30	31		

2019

SEPTEMBER

Sunday 1

Monday 2   Labor Day
Labour Day (Canada)

Tuesday 3

Wednesday 4

Thursday 5

Friday 6

Saturday 7

To-Do List

✓

Shopping List

September 2019

S	M	T	W	TH	F	S
1	2	3	4	5	6	7
8	9	10	11	12	13	14
15	16	17	18	19	20	21
22	23	24	25	26	27	28
29	30					

October 2019

S	M	T	W	TH	F	S
		1	2	3	4	5
6	7	8	9	10	11	12
13	14	15	16	17	18	19
20	21	22	23	24	25	26
27	28	29	30	31		

2019

SEPTEMBER

Sunday 8

Monday 9

Tuesday 10

Wednesday 11

Thursday 12

Friday 13

Saturday 14

To-Do List

✓

Shopping List

September 2019

S	M	T	W	TH	F	S
1	2	3	4	5	6	7
8	9	10	11	12	13	14
15	16	17	18	19	20	21
22	23	24	25	26	27	28
29	30					

October 2019

S	M	T	W	TH	F	S
		1	2	3	4	5
6	7	8	9	10	11	12
13	14	15	16	17	18	19
20	21	22	23	24	25	26
27	28	29	30	31		

2019
SEPTEMBER

Sunday 15

Monday 16

Tuesday 17

Wednesday 18

Thursday 19

Friday 20

Saturday 21

To-Do List

✓	

Shopping List

September 2019

S	M	T	W	TH	F	S
1	2	3	4	5	6	7
8	9	10	11	12	13	14
15	16	17	18	19	20	21
22	23	24	25	26	27	28
29	30					

October 2019

S	M	T	W	TH	F	S
		1	2	3	4	5
6	7	8	9	10	11	12
13	14	15	16	17	18	19
20	21	22	23	24	25	26
27	28	29	30	31		

2019

SEPTEMBER

Sunday 22

Monday 23 First Day of Autumn

Tuesday 24

Wednesday 25

Thursday 26

Friday 27

Saturday 28

To-Do List

✓

Shopping List

September 2019						
S	M	T	W	TH	F	S
1	2	3	4	5	6	7
8	9	10	11	12	13	14
15	16	17	18	19	20	21
22	23	24	25	26	27	28
29	30					

October 2019						
S	M	T	W	TH	F	S
		1	2	3	4	5
6	7	8	9	10	11	12
13	14	15	16	17	18	19
20	21	22	23	24	25	26
27	28	29	30	31		

2019

SEPT-OCT

Sunday 29

Monday 30 Rosh Hashana

Tuesday 1

Wednesday 2

Thursday 3

Friday 4

Saturday 5

To-Do List

✓

Trial by Fire

Blessed is the one who perseveres under trial because, having stood the test, that person will receive the crown of life.

JAMES 1:12

Last winter while visiting a natural history museum in Colorado, I learned some remarkable facts about the aspen tree. An entire grove of slender, white-trunked aspens can grow from a single seed and share the same root system. These root systems can exist for thousands of years whether or not they produce trees. They sleep underground, waiting for fire, flood, or avalanche to clear a space for them in the shady forest. After a natural disaster has cleared the land, aspen roots can sense the sun at last. The roots send up saplings, which become trees.

For aspens, new growth is made possible by the devastation of a natural disaster. James writes that our growth in faith is also made possible by difficulties. "Consider it pure joy," he writes, "whenever you face trials of many kinds, because you know that the testing of your faith produces perseverance. Let perseverance finish its work so that you may be mature and complete, not lacking anything" (James 1:2–4).

It's difficult to be joyful during trials, but we can take hope from the fact that God will use difficult circumstances to help us reach maturity. Like aspen trees, faith can grow in times of trial when difficulty clears space in our hearts for the light of God to touch us.

AMY PETERSON

Thank you, God, for being with us in our trials, and for helping us to grow through difficult circumstances.

Photo: Aspens in San Juan Mountains, Colorado, US © Darrell Gulin

2019

OCTOBER

Sunday	Monday	Tuesday	Wednesday
		1	2
6	7	8	9 Yom Kippur
13	14 First Day of Sukkot Columbus Day/ Indigenous Peoples' Day Thanksgiving Day (Canada)	15	16
20	21	22	23
27	28	29	30

I am God, and there is none like me.
—ISAIAH 46:9

Thursday	Friday	Saturday	Notes
3	4	5	
10	11	12	
17	18	19	
24	25	26	
31			

Shopping List

October 2019

S	M	T	W	TH	F	S
		1	2	3	4	5
6	7	8	9	10	11	12
13	14	15	16	17	18	19
20	21	22	23	24	25	26
27	28	29	30	31		

November 2019

S	M	T	W	TH	F	S
					1	2
3	4	5	6	7	8	9
10	11	12	13	14	15	16
17	18	19	20	21	22	23
24	25	26	27	28	29	30

2019

OCTOBER

Sunday 6

Monday 7

Tuesday 8

Wednesday 9 Yom Kippur

Thursday 10

Friday 11

Saturday 12

To-Do List

Shopping List

October 2019
S	M	T	W	TH	F	S
		1	2	3	4	5
6	7	8	9	10	11	12
13	14	15	16	17	18	19
20	21	22	23	24	25	26
27	28	29	30	31		

November 2019
S	M	T	W	TH	F	S
					1	2
3	4	5	6	7	8	9
10	11	12	13	14	15	16
17	18	19	20	21	22	23
24	25	26	27	28	29	30

2019

OCTOBER

Sunday 13

Monday 14 First Day of Sukkot
Columbus Day/Indigenous Peoples' Day
Thanksgiving Day (Canada)

Tuesday 15

Wednesday 16

Thursday 17

Friday 18

Saturday 19

To-Do List

✓

Shopping List

✓	

October 2019

S	M	T	W	TH	F	S
		1	2	3	4	5
6	7	8	9	10	11	12
13	14	15	16	17	18	19
20	21	22	23	24	25	26
27	28	29	30	31		

November 2019

S	M	T	W	TH	F	S
					1	2
3	4	5	6	7	8	9
10	11	12	13	14	15	16
17	18	19	20	21	22	23
24	25	26	27	28	29	30

2019

OCTOBER

Sunday 20

Monday 21

Tuesday 22

Wednesday 23

Thursday 24

Friday 25

Saturday 26

To-Do List

✓

Shopping List

October 2019
S	M	T	W	TH	F	S
		1	2	3	4	5
6	7	8	9	10	11	12
13	14	15	16	17	18	19
20	21	22	23	24	25	26
27	28	29	30	31		

November 2019
S	M	T	W	TH	F	S
					1	2
3	4	5	6	7	8	9
10	11	12	13	14	15	16
17	18	19	20	21	22	23
24	25	26	27	28	29	30

2019
OCT–NOV

Sunday 27

Monday 28

Tuesday 29

Wednesday 30

Thursday 31

Friday 1

Saturday 2

To-Do List

✓

2019

NOVEMBER

Sunday	Monday	Tuesday	Wednesday
3 Daylight Saving Time Ends	4	5	6
10	11 Veterans Day Remembrance Day (Canada)	12	13
17	18	19	20
24	25	26	27

You open your hand and satisfy the desires of every living thing. —PSALM 145:16

Thursday	Friday	Saturday	Notes
	1	2	
7	8	9	
14	15	16	
21	22	23	
28 Thanksgiving Day	29	30	

November 2019

S	M	T	W	TH	F	S
					1	2
3	4	5	6	7	8	9
10	11	12	13	14	15	16
17	18	19	20	21	22	23
24	25	26	27	28	29	30

December 2019

S	M	T	W	TH	F	S
1	2	3	4	5	6	7
8	9	10	11	12	13	14
15	16	17	18	19	20	21
22	23	24	25	26	27	28
29	30	31				

2019
NOVEMBER

Sunday 3 Daylight Saving Time Ends

Monday 4

Tuesday 5

Wednesday 6

Thursday 7

Friday 8

Saturday 9

To-Do List

✓

Shopping List

✓	

November 2019

S	M	T	W	TH	F	S
					1	2
3	4	5	6	7	8	9
10	11	12	13	14	15	16
17	18	19	20	21	22	23
24	25	26	27	28	29	30

December 2019

S	M	T	W	TH	F	S
1	2	3	4	5	6	7
8	9	10	11	12	13	14
15	16	17	18	19	20	21
22	23	24	25	26	27	28
29	30	31				

2019
NOVEMBER

Sunday 10

Monday 11 — Veterans Day
Remembrance Day (Canada)

Tuesday 12

Wednesday 13

Thursday 14

Friday 15

Saturday 16

To-Do List

✓

November 2019								December 2019						
S	M	T	W	TH	F	S		S	M	T	W	TH	F	S
					1	2		1	2	3	4	5	6	7
3	4	5	6	7	8	9		8	9	10	11	12	13	14
10	11	12	13	14	15	16		15	16	17	18	19	20	21
17	18	19	20	21	22	23		22	23	24	25	26	27	28
24	25	26	27	28	29	30		29	30	31				

Shopping List

2019

NOVEMBER

Sunday 17

Monday 18

Tuesday 19

Wednesday 20

Thursday 21

Friday 22

Saturday 23

To-Do List

✓

Shopping List

November 2019

S	M	T	W	TH	F	S
					1	2
3	4	5	6	7	8	9
10	11	12	13	14	15	16
17	18	19	20	21	22	23
24	25	26	27	28	29	30

December 2019

S	M	T	W	TH	F	S
1	2	3	4	5	6	7
8	9	10	11	12	13	14
15	16	17	18	19	20	21
22	23	24	25	26	27	28
29	30	31				

2019

NOVEMBER

Sunday 24

Monday 25

Tuesday 26

Wednesday 27

Thursday 28 Thanksgiving Day

Friday 29

Saturday 30

To-Do List

✓

2019

DECEMBER

Sunday	Monday	Tuesday	Wednesday
1 Advent Begins	2	3	4
8	9	10	11
15	16	17	18
22	23 First Day of Hanukkah	24 Christmas Eve	25 Christmas Day
29	30 Hanukkah ends	31 New Year's Eve	

Now, our God, we give you thanks, and praise your glorious name. —1 CHRONICLES 29:13

Thursday	Friday	Saturday	Notes
5	6	7	
12	13	14	
19	20	21 First Day of Winter	
26 Boxing Day (Canada)	27	28	

Shopping List

December 2019

S	M	T	W	TH	F	S
1	2	3	4	5	6	7
8	9	10	11	12	13	14
15	16	17	18	19	20	21
22	23	24	25	26	27	28
29	30	31				

January 2020

S	M	T	W	TH	F	S
			1	2	3	4
5	6	7	8	9	10	11
12	13	14	15	16	17	18
19	20	21	22	23	24	25
26	27	28	29	30	31	

2019

DECEMBER

Sunday 1 Advent Begins

Monday 2

Tuesday 3

Wednesday 4

Thursday 5

Friday 6

Saturday 7

To-Do List

✓

Shopping List

December 2019

S	M	T	W	TH	F	S
1	2	3	4	5	6	7
8	9	10	11	12	13	14
15	16	17	18	19	20	21
22	23	24	25	26	27	28
29	30	31				

January 2020

S	M	T	W	TH	F	S
			1	2	3	4
5	6	7	8	9	10	11
12	13	14	15	16	17	18
19	20	21	22	23	24	25
26	27	28	29	30	31	

2019

DECEMBER

Sunday 8

Monday 9

Tuesday 10

Wednesday 11

Thursday 12

Friday 13

Saturday 14

To-Do List

Shopping List

December 2019

S	M	T	W	TH	F	S
1	2	3	4	5	6	7
8	9	10	11	12	13	14
15	16	17	18	19	20	21
22	23	24	25	26	27	28
29	30	31				

January 2020

S	M	T	W	TH	F	S
			1	2	3	4
5	6	7	8	9	10	11
12	13	14	15	16	17	18
19	20	21	22	23	24	25
26	27	28	29	30	31	

2019

DECEMBER

Sunday 15

Monday 16

Tuesday 17

Wednesday 18

Thursday 19

Friday 20

Saturday 21 First Day of Winter

To-Do List

✓

Shopping List

December 2019

S	M	T	W	TH	F	S
1	2	3	4	5	6	7
8	9	10	11	12	13	14
15	16	17	18	19	20	21
22	23	24	25	26	27	28
29	30	31				

January 2020

S	M	T	W	TH	F	S
			1	2	3	4
5	6	7	8	9	10	11
12	13	14	15	16	17	18
19	20	21	22	23	24	25
26	27	28	29	30	31	

2019
DECEMBER

Sunday 22

Monday 23 First Day of Hanukkah

Tuesday 24 Christmas Eve

Wednesday 25   Christmas Day

Thursday 26   Boxing Day (Canada)

Friday 27

Saturday 28

To-Do List

✓

Shopping List

December 2019

S	M	T	W	TH	F	S
1	2	3	4	5	6	7
8	9	10	11	12	13	14
15	16	17	18	19	20	21
22	23	24	25	26	27	28
29	30	31				

January 2020

S	M	T	W	TH	F	S
			1	2	3	4
5	6	7	8	9	10	11
12	13	14	15	16	17	18
19	20	21	22	23	24	25
26	27	28	29	30	31	

2019–2020

DEC–JAN

Sunday 29

Monday 30 Hanukkah ends

Tuesday 31 New Year's Eve

Wednesday 1 New Year's Day

Thursday 2

Friday 3

Saturday 4

To-Do List

✓

Bible Reading Schedule

JANUARY

1   Gen. 1–3; Mt. 1
2   Gen. 4–6; Mt. 2
3   Gen. 7–9; Mt. 3
4   Gen. 10–12; Mt. 4
5   Gen. 13–15; Mt. 5:1-26
6   Gen. 16–17; Mt. 5:27-48
7   Gen. 18–19; Mt. 6:1-18
8   Gen. 20–22; Mt. 6:19-34
9   Gen. 23–24; Mt. 7
10   Gen. 25–26; Mt. 8:1-17
11   Gen. 27–28; Mt. 8:18-34
12   Gen. 29–30; Mt. 9:1-17
13   Gen. 31–32; Mt. 9:18-38
14   Gen. 33–35; Mt. 10:1-20
15   Gen. 36–38; Mt. 10:21-42
16   Gen. 39–40; Mt. 11
17   Gen. 41–42; Mt. 12:1-23
18   Gen. 43–45; Mt. 12:24-50
19   Gen. 46–48; Mt. 13:1-30
20   Gen. 49–50; Mt. 13:31-58
21   Ex. 1–3; Mt. 14:1-21
22   Ex. 4–6; Mt. 14:22-36
23   Ex. 7–8; Mt. 15:1-20
24   Ex. 9–11; Mt. 15:21-39
25   Ex. 12–13; Mt. 16
26   Ex. 14–15; Mt. 17
27   Ex. 16–18; Mt. 18:1-20
28   Ex. 19–20; Mt. 18:21-35
29   Ex. 21–22; Mt. 19
30   Ex. 23–24; Mt. 20:1-16
31   Ex. 25–26; Mt. 20:17-34

FEBRUARY

1   Ex. 27–28; Mt. 21:1-22
2   Ex. 29–30; Mt. 21:23-46
3   Ex. 31–33; Mt. 22:1-22
4   Ex. 34–35; Mt. 22:23-46
5   Ex. 36–38; Mt. 23:1-22
6   Ex. 39–40; Mt. 23:23-39
7   Lev. 1–3; Mt. 24:1-28
8   Lev. 4–5; Mt. 24:29-51
9   Lev. 6–7; Mt. 25:1-30
10   Lev. 8–10; Mt. 25:31-46
11   Lev. 11–12; Mt. 26:1-25
12   Lev. 13; Mt. 26:26-50
13   Lev. 14; Mt. 26:51-75
14   Lev. 15–16; Mt. 27:1-26
15   Lev. 17–18; Mt. 27:27-50
16   Lev. 19–20; Mt. 27:51-66
17   Lev. 21–22; Mt. 28
18   Lev. 23–24; Mk. 1:1-22
19   Lev. 25; Mk. 1:23-45
20   Lev. 26–27; Mk. 2
21   Num. 1–3; Mk. 3
22   Num. 4–6; Mk. 4:1-20
23   Num. 7–8; Mk. 4:21-41
24   Num. 9–11; Mk. 5:1-20
25   Num. 12–14; Mk. 5:21-43
26   Num. 15–16; Mk. 6:1-29
27   Num. 17–19; Mk. 6:30-56
28   Num. 20–22; Mk. 7:1-13

MARCH

1   Num. 23–25; Mk. 7:14-37
2   Num. 26–27; Mk. 8:1-21
3   Num. 28–30; Mk. 8:22-38
4   Num. 31–33; Mk. 9:1-29
5   Num. 34–36; Mk. 9:30-50
6   Dt. 1–2; Mk. 10:1-31
7   Dt. 3–4; Mk. 10:32-52
8   Dt. 5–7; Mk. 11:1-18
9   Dt. 8–10; Mk. 11:19-33
10   Dt. 11–13; Mk. 12:1-27
11   Dt. 14–16; Mk. 12:28-44
12   Dt. 17–19; Mk. 13:1-20
13   Dt. 20–22; Mk. 13:21-37
14   Dt. 23–25; Mk. 14:1-26
15   Dt. 26–27; Mk. 14:27-53
16   Dt. 28–29; Mk. 14:54-72
17   Dt. 30–31; Mk. 15:1-25
18   Dt. 32–34; Mk. 15:26-47
19   Josh. 1–3; Mk. 16
20   Josh. 4–6; Lk. 1:1-20
21   Josh. 7–9; Lk. 1:21-38
22   Josh. 10–12; Lk. 1:39-56
23   Josh. 13–15; Lk. 1:57-80
24   Josh. 16–18; Lk. 2:1-24
25   Josh. 19–21; Lk. 2:25-52
26   Josh. 22–24; Lk. 3
27   Jud. 1–3; Lk. 4:1-30
28   Jud. 4–6; Lk. 4:31-44
29   Jud. 7–8; Lk. 5:1-16
30   Jud. 9–10; Lk. 5:17-39
31   Jud. 11–12; Lk. 6:1-26

Bible Reading Schedule

APRIL

- 1   Jud. 13–15; Lk. 6:27-49
- 2   Jud. 16–18; Lk. 7:1-30
- 3   Jud. 19–21; Lk. 7:31-50
- 4   Ruth 1–4; Lk. 8:1-25
- 5   1 Sam. 1–3; Lk. 8:26-56
- 6   1 Sam. 4–6; Lk. 9:1-17
- 7   1 Sam. 7–9; Lk. 9:18-36
- 8   1 Sam. 10–12; Lk. 9:37-62
- 9   1 Sam. 13–14; Lk. 10:1-24
- 10   1 Sam. 15–16; Lk. 10:25-42
- 11   1 Sam. 17–18; Lk. 11:1-28
- 12   1 Sam. 19–21; Lk. 11:29-54
- 13   1 Sam. 22–24; Lk. 12:1-31
- 14   1 Sam. 25–26; Lk. 12:32-59
- 15   1 Sam. 27–29; Lk. 13:1-22
- 16   1 Sam. 30–31; Lk. 13:23-35
- 17   2 Sam. 1–2; Lk. 14:1-24
- 18   2 Sam. 3–5; Lk. 14:25-35
- 19   2 Sam. 6–8; Lk. 15:1-10
- 20   2 Sam. 9–11; Lk. 15:11-32
- 21   2 Sam. 12–13; Lk. 16
- 22   2 Sam. 14–15; Lk. 17:1-19
- 23   2 Sam. 16–18; Lk. 17:20-37
- 24   2 Sam. 19–20; Lk. 18:1-23
- 25   2 Sam. 21–22; Lk. 18:24-43
- 26   2 Sam. 23–24; Lk. 19:1-27
- 27   1 Ki. 1–2; Lk. 19:28-48
- 28   1 Ki. 3–5; Lk. 20:1-26
- 29   1 Ki. 6–7; Lk. 20:27-47
- 30   1 Ki. 8–9; Lk. 21:1-19

MAY

- 1   1 Ki. 10–11; Lk. 21:20-38
- 2   1 Ki. 12–13; Lk. 22:1-20
- 3   1 Ki. 14–15; Lk. 22:21-46
- 4   1 Ki. 16–18; Lk. 22:47-71
- 5   1 Ki. 19–20; Lk. 23:1-25
- 6   1 Ki. 21–22; Lk. 23:26-56
- 7   2 Ki. 1–3; Lk. 24:1-35
- 8   2 Ki. 4–6; Lk. 24:36-53
- 9   2 Ki. 7–9; Jn. 1:1-28
- 10   2 Ki. 10–12; Jn. 1:29-51
- 11   2 Ki. 13–14; Jn. 2
- 12   2 Ki. 15–16; Jn. 3:1-18
- 13   2 Ki. 17–18; Jn. 3:19-36
- 14   2 Ki. 19–21; Jn. 4:1-30
- 15   2 Ki. 22–23; Jn. 4:31-54
- 16   2 Ki. 24–25; Jn. 5:1-24

- 17   1 Chr. 1–3; Jn. 5:25-47
- 18   1 Chr. 4–6; Jn. 6:1-21
- 19   1 Chr. 7–9; Jn. 6:22-44
- 20   1 Chr. 10–12; Jn. 6:45-71
- 21   1 Chr. 13–15; Jn. 7:1-27
- 22   1 Chr. 16–18; Jn. 7:28-53
- 23   1 Chr. 19–21; Jn. 8:1-27
- 24   1 Chr. 22–24; Jn. 8:28-59
- 25   1 Chr. 25–27; Jn. 9:1-23
- 26   1 Chr. 28–29; Jn. 9:24-41
- 27   2 Chr. 1–3; Jn. 10:1-23
- 28   2 Chr. 4–6; Jn. 10:24-42
- 29   2 Chr. 7–9; Jn. 11:1-29
- 30   2 Chr. 10–12; Jn. 11:30-57
- 31   2 Chr. 13–14; Jn. 12:1-26

JUNE

- 1   2 Chr. 15–16; Jn. 12:27-50
- 2   2 Chr. 17–18; Jn. 13:1-20
- 3   2 Chr. 19–20; Jn. 13:21-38
- 4   2 Chr. 21–22; Jn. 14
- 5   2 Chr. 23–24; Jn. 15
- 6   2 Chr. 25–27; Jn. 16
- 7   2 Chr. 28–29; Jn. 17
- 8   2 Chr. 30–31; Jn. 18:1-18
- 9   2 Chr. 32–33; Jn. 18:19-40
- 10   2 Chr. 34–36; Jn. 19:1-22
- 11   Ezra 1–2; Jn. 19:23-42
- 12   Ezra 3–5; Jn. 20
- 13   Ezra 6–8; Jn. 21
- 14   Ezra 9–10; Acts 1
- 15   Neh. 1–3; Acts 2:1-21
- 16   Neh. 4–6; Acts 2:22-47
- 17   Neh. 7–9; Acts 3
- 18   Neh. 10–11; Acts 4:1-22
- 19   Neh. 12–13; Acts 4:23-37
- 20   Est. 1–2; Acts 5:1-21
- 21   Est. 3–5; Acts 5:22-42
- 22   Est. 6–8; Acts 6
- 23   Est. 9–10; Acts 7:1-21
- 24   Job 1–2; Acts 7:22-43
- 25   Job 3–4; Acts 7:44-60
- 26   Job 5–7; Acts 8:1-25
- 27   Job 8–10; Acts 8:26-40
- 28   Job 11–13; Acts 9:1-21
- 29   Job 14–16; Acts 9:22-43
- 30   Job 17–19; Acts 10:1-23

Bible Reading Schedule

JULY

1   Job 20–21; Acts 10:24-48
2   Job 22–24; Acts 11
3   Job 25–27; Acts 12
4   Job 28–29; Acts 13:1-25
5   Job 30–31; Acts 13:26-52
6   Job 32–33; Acts 14
7   Job 34–35; Acts 15:1-21
8   Job 36–37; Acts 15:22-41
9   Job 38–40; Acts 16:1-21
10   Job 41–42; Acts 16:22-40
11   Ps. 1–3; Acts 17:1-15
12   Ps. 4–6; Acts 17:16-34
13   Ps. 7–9; Acts 18
14   Ps. 10–12; Acts 19:1-20
15   Ps. 13–15; Acts 19:21-41
16   Ps. 16–17; Acts 20:1-16
17   Ps. 18–19; Acts 20:17-38
18   Ps. 20–22; Acts 21:1-17
19   Ps. 23–25; Acts 21:18-40
20   Ps. 26–28; Acts 22
21   Ps. 29–30; Acts 23:1-15
22   Ps. 31–32; Acts 23:16-35
23   Ps. 33–34; Acts 24
24   Ps. 35–36; Acts 25
25   Ps. 37–39; Acts 26
26   Ps. 40–42; Acts 27:1-26
27   Ps. 43–45; Acts 27:27-44
28   Ps. 46–48; Acts 28
29   Ps. 49–50; Rom. 1
30   Ps. 51–53; Rom. 2
31   Ps. 54–56; Rom. 3

AUGUST

1   Ps. 57–59; Rom. 4
2   Ps. 60–62; Rom. 5
3   Ps. 63–65; Rom. 6
4   Ps. 66–67; Rom. 7
5   Ps. 68–69; Rom. 8:1-21
6   Ps. 70–71; Rom. 8:22-39
7   Ps. 72–73; Rom. 9:1-15
8   Ps. 74–76; Rom. 9:16-33
9   Ps. 77–78; Rom. 10
10   Ps. 79–80; Rom. 11:1-18
11   Ps. 81–83; Rom. 11:19-36
12   Ps. 84–86; Rom. 12
13   Ps. 87–88; Rom. 13
14   Ps. 89–90; Rom. 14
15   Ps. 91–93; Rom. 15:1-13

16   Ps. 94–96; Rom. 15:14-33
17   Ps. 97–99; Rom. 16
18   Ps. 100–102; 1 Cor. 1
19   Ps. 103–104; 1 Cor. 2
20   Ps. 105–106; 1 Cor. 3
21   Ps. 107–109; 1 Cor. 4
22   Ps. 110–112; 1 Cor. 5
23   Ps. 113–115; 1 Cor. 6
24   Ps. 116–118; 1 Cor. 7:1-19
25   Ps. 119:1-88; 1 Cor. 7:20-40
26   Ps. 119:89-176; 1 Cor. 8
27   Ps. 120–122; 1 Cor. 9
28   Ps. 123–125; 1 Cor. 10:1-18
29   Ps. 126–128; 1 Cor. 10:19-33
30   Ps. 129–131; 1 Cor. 11:1-16
31   Ps. 132–134; 1 Cor. 11:17-34

SEPTEMBER

1   Ps. 135–136; 1 Cor. 12
2   Ps. 137–139; 1 Cor. 13
3   Ps. 140–142; 1 Cor. 14:1-20
4   Ps. 143–145; 1 Cor. 14:21-40
5   Ps. 146–147; 1 Cor. 15:1-28
6   Ps. 148–150; 1 Cor. 15:29-58
7   Prov. 1–2; 1 Cor. 16
8   Prov. 3–5; 2 Cor. 1
9   Prov. 6–7; 2 Cor. 2
10   Prov. 8–9; 2 Cor. 3
11   Prov. 10–12; 2 Cor. 4
12   Prov. 13–15; 2 Cor. 5
13   Prov. 16–18; 2 Cor. 6
14   Prov. 19–21; 2 Cor. 7
15   Prov. 22–24; 2 Cor. 8
16   Prov. 25–26; 2 Cor. 9
17   Prov. 27–29; 2 Cor. 10
18   Prov. 30–31; 2 Cor. 11:1-15
19   Eccl. 1–3; 2 Cor. 11:16-33
20   Eccl. 4–6; 2 Cor. 12
21   Eccl. 7–9; 2 Cor. 13
22   Eccl. 10–12; Gal. 1
23   Song 1–3; Gal. 2
24   Song 4–5; Gal. 3
25   Song 6–8; Gal. 4
26   Isa. 1–2; Gal. 5
27   Isa. 3–4; Gal. 6
28   Isa. 5–6; Eph. 1
29   Isa. 7–8; Eph. 2
30   Isa. 9–10; Eph. 3

Bible Reading Schedule

OCTOBER

1   Isa. 11–13; Eph. 4
2   Isa. 14–16; Eph. 5:1-16
3   Isa. 17–19; Eph. 5:17-33
4   Isa. 20–22; Eph. 6
5   Isa. 23–25; Phil. 1
6   Isa. 26–27; Phil. 2
7   Isa. 28–29; Phil. 3
8   Isa. 30–31; Phil 4
9   Isa. 32–33; Col. 1
10 Isa. 34–36; Col. 2
11 Isa. 37–38; Col. 3
12 Isa. 39–40; Col. 4
13 Isa. 41–42; 1 Th. 1
14 Isa. 43–44; 1 Th. 2
15 Isa. 45–46; 1 Th. 3
16 Isa. 47–49; 1 Th. 4
17 Isa. 50–52; 1 Th. 5
18 Isa. 53–55; 2 Th. 1
19 Isa. 56–58; 2 Th. 2
20 Isa. 59–61; 2 Th. 3
21 Isa. 62–64; 1 Tim. 1
22 Isa. 65–66; 1 Tim. 2
23 Jer. 1–2; 1 Tim. 3
24 Jer. 3–5; 1 Tim. 4
25 Jer. 6–8; 1 Tim. 5
26 Jer. 9–11; 1 Tim. 6
27 Jer. 12–14; 2 Tim. 1
28 Jer. 15–17; 2 Tim. 2
29 Jer. 18–19; 2 Tim. 3
30 Jer. 20–21; 2 Tim. 4
31 Jer. 22–23; Ti. 1

NOVEMBER

1   Jer. 24–26; Ti. 2
2   Jer. 27–29; Ti. 3
3   Jer. 30–31; Philemon
4   Jer. 32–33; Heb. 1
5   Jer. 34–36; Heb. 2
6   Jer. 37–39; Heb. 3
7   Jer. 40–42; Heb. 4
8   Jer. 43–45; Heb. 5
9   Jer. 46–47; Heb. 6
10 Jer. 48–49; Heb. 7
11 Jer. 50; Heb. 8
12 Jer. 51–52; Heb. 9
13 Lam. 1–2; Heb. 10:1-18
14 Lam. 3–5; Heb. 10:19-39
15 Ezek. 1–2; Heb. 11:1-19
16 Ezek. 3–4; Heb. 11:20-40
17 Ezek. 5–7; Heb. 12
18 Ezek. 8–10; Heb. 13
19 Ezek. 11–13; Jas. 1
20 Ezek. 14–15; Jas. 2
21 Ezek. 16–17; Jas. 3
22 Ezek. 18–19; Jas. 4
23 Ezek. 20–21; Jas. 5
24 Ezek. 22–23; 1 Pet. 1
25 Ezek. 24–26; 1 Pet. 2
26 Ezek. 27–29; 1 Pet. 3
27 Ezek. 30–32; 1 Pet. 4
28 Ezek. 33–34; 1 Pet. 5
29 Ezek. 35–36; 2 Pet. 1
30 Ezek. 37–39; 2 Pet. 2

DECEMBER

1   Ezek. 40–41; 2 Pet. 3
2   Ezek. 42–44; 1 Jn. 1
3   Ezek. 45–46; 1 Jn. 2
4   Ezek. 47–48; 1 Jn. 3
5   Dan. 1–2; 1 Jn. 4
6   Dan. 3–4; 1 Jn. 5
7   Dan. 5–7; 2 John
8   Dan. 8–10; 3 John
9   Dan. 11–12; Jude
10 Hos. 1–4; Rev. 1
11 Hos. 5–8; Rev. 2
12 Hos. 9–11; Rev. 3
13 Hos. 12–14; Rev. 4
14 Joel 1–3; Rev. 5
15 Amos 1–3; Rev. 6
16 Amos 4–6; Rev. 7
17 Amos 7–9; Rev. 8
18 Obadiah; Rev. 9
19 Jonah 1–4; Rev. 10
20 Mic. 1–3; Rev. 11
21 Mic. 4–5; Rev. 12
22 Mic. 6–7; Rev. 13
23 Nahum 1–3; Rev. 14
24 Habakkuk 1–3; Rev. 15
25 Zephaniah 1–3; Rev. 16
26 Haggai 1–2; Rev. 17
27 Zech. 1–4; Rev. 18
28 Zech. 5–8; Rev. 19
29 Zech. 9–12; Rev. 20
30 Zech. 13–14; Rev. 21
31 Malachi 1–4; Rev. 22

NOTES

NOTES

NOTES

NOTES

NOTES

NOTES

IMPORTANT CONTACTS

Name:

Address:

City: State: Zip:

Home Phone: Work Phone:

Email: Cell Phone:

Additional Information:

....

Name:

Address:

City: State: Zip:

Home Phone: Work Phone:

Email: Cell Phone:

Additional Information:

....

Name:

Address:

City: State: Zip:

Home Phone: Work Phone:

Email: Cell Phone:

Additional Information:

....

Name:

Address:

City: State: Zip:

Home Phone: Work Phone:

Email: Cell Phone:

Additional Information:

IMPORTANT CONTACTS

Name:

Address:

City: State: Zip:

Home Phone: Work Phone:

Email: Cell Phone:

Additional Information:

Name:

Address:

City: State: Zip:

Home Phone: Work Phone:

Email: Cell Phone:

Additional Information:

Name:

Address:

City: State: Zip:

Home Phone: Work Phone:

Email: Cell Phone:

Additional Information:

Name:

Address:

City: State: Zip:

Home Phone: Work Phone:

Email: Cell Phone:

Additional Information:

IMPORTANT CONTACTS

Name:

Address:

City: State: Zip:

Home Phone: Work Phone:

Email: Cell Phone:

Additional Information:

Name:

Address:

City: State: Zip:

Home Phone: Work Phone:

Email: Cell Phone:

Additional Information:

Name:

Address:

City: State: Zip:

Home Phone: Work Phone:

Email: Cell Phone:

Additional Information:

Name:

Address:

City: State: Zip:

Home Phone: Work Phone:

Email: Cell Phone:

Additional Information:

IMPORTANT CONTACTS

Name:

Address:

City: State: Zip:

Home Phone: Work Phone:

Email: Cell Phone:

Additional Information:

Name:

Address:

City: State: Zip:

Home Phone: Work Phone:

Email: Cell Phone:

Additional Information:

Name:

Address:

City: State: Zip:

Home Phone: Work Phone:

Email: Cell Phone:

Additional Information:

Name:

Address:

City: State: Zip:

Home Phone: Work Phone:

Email: Cell Phone:

Additional Information:

IMPORTANT CONTACTS

Name:

Address:

City: State: Zip:

Home Phone: Work Phone:

Email: Cell Phone:

Additional Information:

Name:

Address:

City: State: Zip:

Home Phone: Work Phone:

Email: Cell Phone:

Additional Information:

Name:

Address:

City: State: Zip:

Home Phone: Work Phone:

Email: Cell Phone:

Additional Information:

Name:

Address:

City: State: Zip:

Home Phone: Work Phone:

Email: Cell Phone:

Additional Information:

IMPORTANT CONTACTS

Name:

Address:

City: State: Zip:

Home Phone: Work Phone:

Email: Cell Phone:

Additional Information:

Name:

Address:

City: State: Zip:

Home Phone: Work Phone:

Email: Cell Phone:

Additional Information:

Name:

Address:

City: State: Zip:

Home Phone: Work Phone:

Email: Cell Phone:

Additional Information:

Name:

Address:

City: State: Zip:

Home Phone: Work Phone:

Email: Cell Phone:

Additional Information:

IMPORTANT CONTACTS

Name:

Address:

City: State: Zip:

Home Phone: Work Phone:

Email: Cell Phone:

Additional Information:

Name:

Address:

City: State: Zip:

Home Phone: Work Phone:

Email: Cell Phone:

Additional Information:

Name:

Address:

City: State: Zip:

Home Phone: Work Phone:

Email: Cell Phone:

Additional Information:

Name:

Address:

City: State: Zip:

Home Phone: Work Phone:

Email: Cell Phone:

Additional Information:

IMPORTANT CONTACTS

Name:

Address:

City: State: Zip:

Home Phone: Work Phone:

Email: Cell Phone:

Additional Information:

Name:

Address:

City: State: Zip:

Home Phone: Work Phone:

Email: Cell Phone:

Additional Information:

Name:

Address:

City: State: Zip:

Home Phone: Work Phone:

Email: Cell Phone:

Additional Information:

Name:

Address:

City: State: Zip:

Home Phone: Work Phone:

Email: Cell Phone:

Additional Information:

HELPING YOU CONNECT WITH GOD EVERY DAY

You can receive your daily devotional by mail, email, web, app, or e-book. *Sign up today!*

odb.org/subscribe